MEADOWS SCHOOL

Can You Make a Pattern?

Lin Picou

Rourke
Educational Media
rourkeeducationalmedia.com

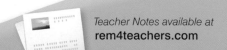

www.rourkeeducationalmedia.com

PHOTO CREDITS: Cover: © Title page: © Robert Harris; page 3: © kali9; page 10: © Perytskyy, © Samuray; page 11: © the-moog; pages 5, 12: © Oksana Petrova, © ajm73; page 13: © xjben; page 14: © GlobalP, © Prapass Wannapinij; page 15: © absolutely_frenchy; page 16, 19: © alxpin; page 17: © stane_c, © rvbox; page 18: © Krasyuk, © Eric IsselÃƒÂ©e; page 20, 21: © Antagain, © eli_asenova; page 22: © Jani Bryson

Edited by Precious McKenzie

Cover and Interior page design by Teri Intzegian

Library of Congress PCN Data

Can You Make a Pattern? / Lin Picou
(Little World Math)
ISBN 978-1-61810-072-6 (hard cover)(alk. paper)
ISBN 978-1-61810-205-8 (soft cover)
Library of Congress Control Number: 2011944370

Rourke Educational Media
Printed in the United States of America,
North Mankato, Minnesota

rourkeeducationalmedia.com
customerservice@rourkeeducationalmedia.com • PO Box 643328 Vero Beach, Florida 32964

Can you make a pattern?

A pattern is a design that repeats over and over again.

You can make a pattern using colored paper clips.

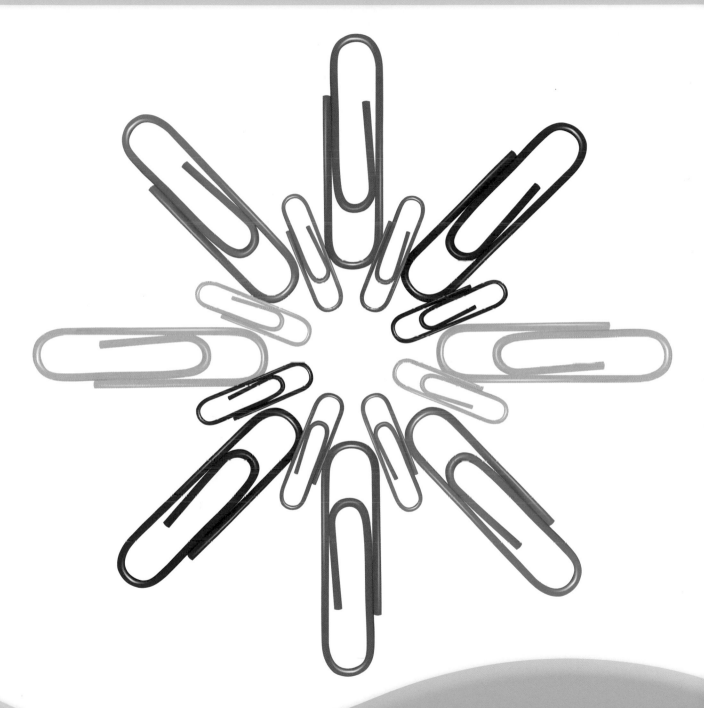

You can change the pattern when you rearrange the colors.

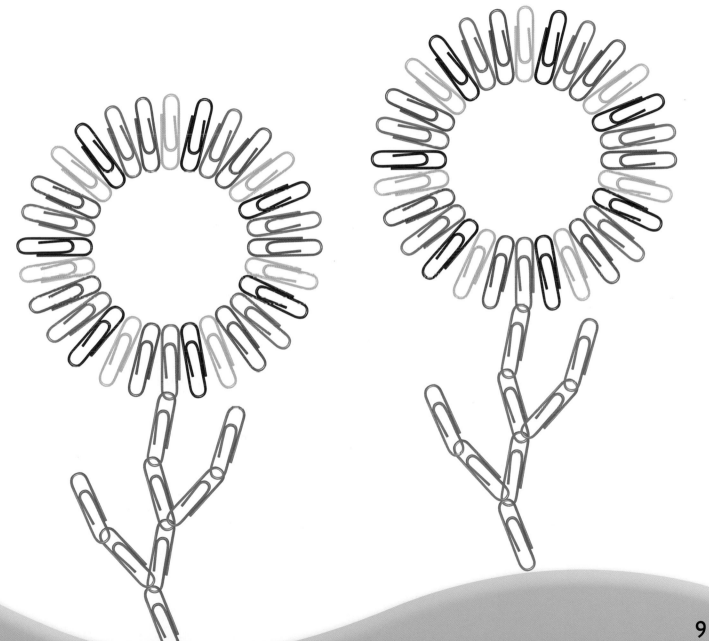

Some patterns use shapes. Can you see patterns made with shapes?

CHECKERBOARD

SOCCER BALL

RACE FLAG

Other patterns use lines.

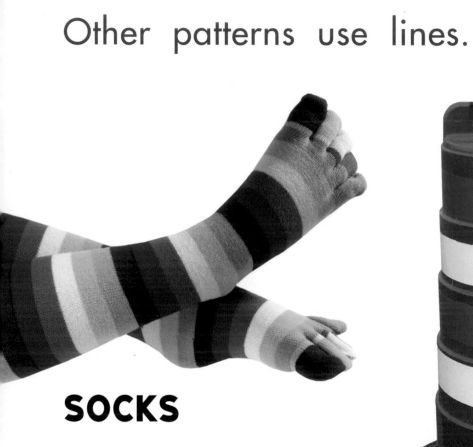

SOCKS

ROAD BARREL

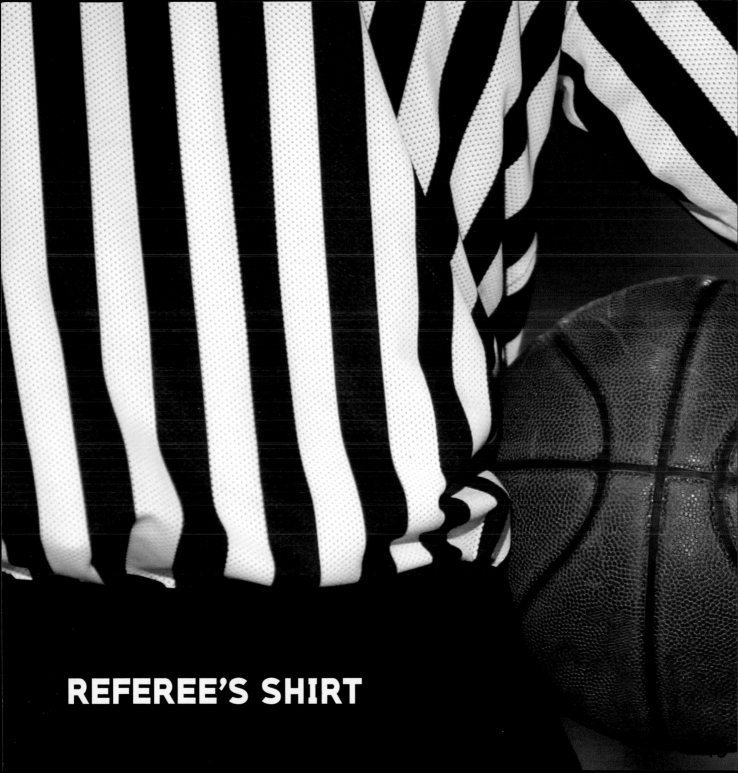

REFEREE'S SHIRT

Animals have patterns, too. How are these patterns alike?

ZEBRA

SKUNK

TIGER

Can you guess which animals wear these patterns?

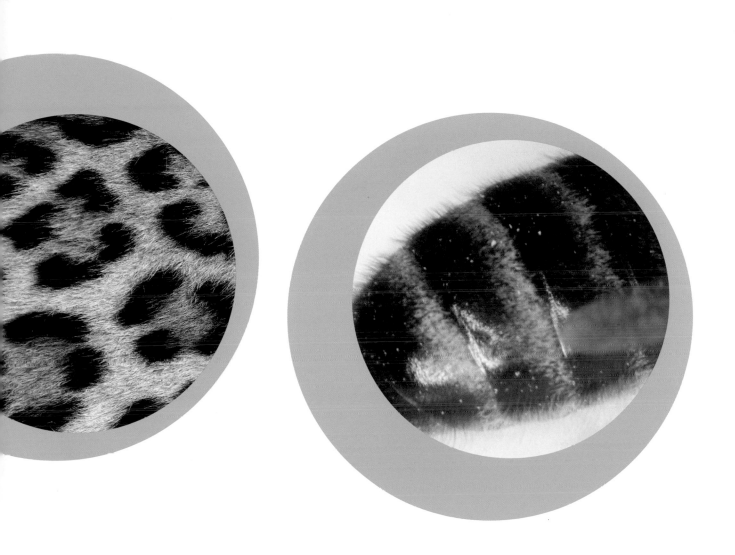

Turn the page to see if you are right!

BEE

LEOPARD

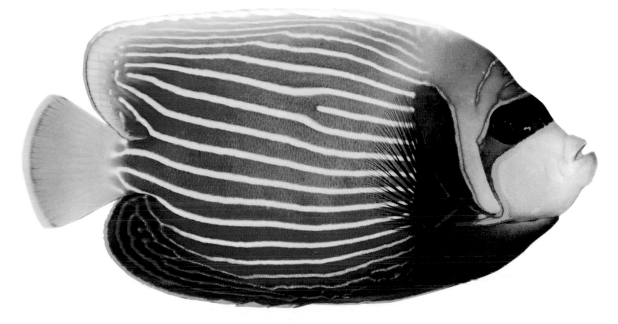

ANGELFISH

You can find patterns almost everywhere!

What comes next in this pattern?

Yes! It's an acorn.

Now it's your turn.

What patterns can you make?

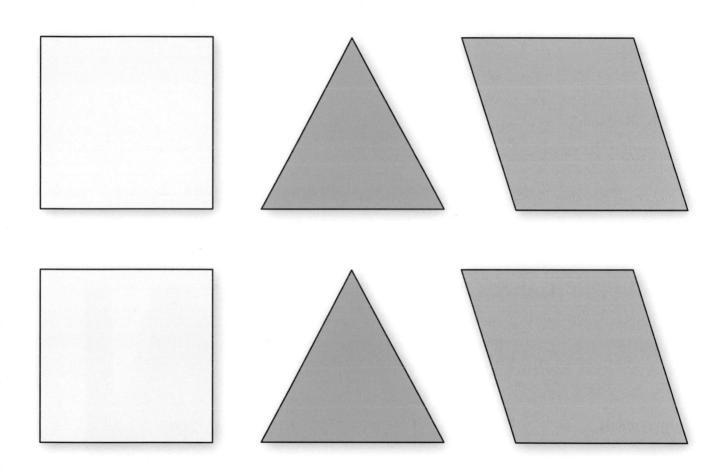

Index

Websites

www.activityvillage.co.uk/dice_games.htm

funschool.kaboose.com/preschool/learn-abcs/games

pbskids.org/cyberchase/math-games/cyber-pattern-player

About the Author

Lin Picou notices the colorful patterns on the butterflies' wings as they visit her garden flowers looking for lunch. Butterflies can't bite you because they have no teeth!

Ask The Author!
www.rem4students.com